BREAKING
THE CYCLE

FREE YOURSELF FROM THE STORY
THAT'S HOLDING YOU BACK

JENNY SCHATZLE

Breaking the Cycle / Jenny Schatzle. —1st ed.

ISBN 978-1-64184-209-9 (pbk)

ISBN 978-1-64184-210-5 (eBook)

Table of Contents

Introduction v

1 Rock Bottom 1

2 Your Parents' Relationship 15

3 Where Our Story Started 23

4 Peer Pressure 29

5 Confronting Your Pain Person 37

6 Food and Body Obsession 47

7 Adult Peer Pressure 55

8 Abusive Boyfriend 63

9 Finding My Career 71

10 You Can't Change for Other People 79

11 Double Life 87

12 The Man Who Changed My Life 95

13 Nobody's Perfect 103

14 Acknowledging the Problem 109

15 Starting a New Life 117

16 Coming into My Own 125

17 Doing the Work Changes Everything 133

18 Moving Forward 141

19 Thank You 147

Acknowledgements 149

About the Author 151

Introduction

This isn't a book where I'm going to tell you what to do with your life. Honestly, what you do with your life is up to you! What I am going to tell you is a brutally honest story about my own life, in case it might help you with yours. How I went from an insecure, self-sabotaging alcoholic with daddy issues, food issues, body issues and self-worth issues, to a successful, strong, confident business owner. I am also going to share about how I became a powerful woman who took back control of her life. The chapters in this book are raw stories and examples from my life. My struggles and successes, and how I worked hard to change it all.

Now, along with sharing my story, I invite you to

do your own work and start changing the conversation for yourself. Let's be honest, if you weren't looking for a change, you probably would not have picked up this book. In order to make a real change, it's going to take some conversation. This book is about being open and honest with yourself and everything you have been through in your life. It's about getting to the root of where it all started and changing your story, your self-talk, your relationships, and your outlook on who you are and the life you are living.

At the end of every chapter, I ask you three questions about YOU in order to help you do your own work and start a different conversation. My goal with this book is that you read my story, and in some way, relate and reflect on your own life. There will be some chapters that hit you like a ton of bricks, and some that you may not connect with, and that is okay.

While doing this reading and work, I highly suggest creating a space where you are able to read and write with no judgement; where you feel comfortable and authentic in what you are writing. The result of creating a space for yourself can be that you are more creative, you become more in touch with your emotions, and you are able to write more freely. As an example, here are three ways to create a space to do the work:

Create a time of day that works best for you

For some, it is first thing in the morning. For others it's before bed. I like to journal and read first thing in the morning. I know many people who prefer to do it at night, after putting the kids to sleep, or right before going to bed. Pick a time that works best for you, but also allow yourself to be flexible.

Create a physical space

Find somewhere quiet and private where you can focus for 15-30 minutes. If you have an office in your house, or maybe the kitchen table. Light a candle or get your favorite blanket. A lot of people say it's not good to work in bed, but I love it. My favorite space is sitting up in bed. It is where I meditate, journal, and read for thirty minutes before my day starts or before I go to bed. Again, it's wherever you find peace and comfort to be your most creative and honest. This is also a place you can feel safe to write without judgement.

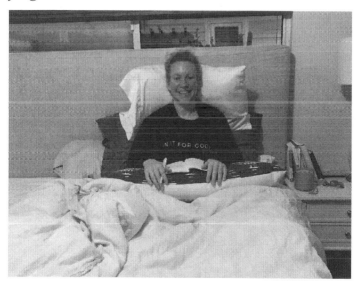

Picture my husband took of me journaling in bed

Create a phone-free zone while doing the work

Our phones can be distracting. When we are connected with our phones, we are disconnected from ourselves. Shut off your phone or put it into another room while you do the work.

Make your workspace even more enjoyable by adding light classical or mellow music, and nice lighting. Also, setting an alarm and committing to working for a specific timeframe can help keep you focused. Set the timer on your phone for however long you'd like and place it out of reach until the timer goes off.

I am honest and open with you about my life in hopes that you will be honest and open with yourself and what you are struggling with. I find if we are vulnerable and transparent, that is where real change can happen. I want you to know I am someone who believes that if I can change my life, anyone can change theirs. You just have to be willing to do the work and get ready to take the leap into your most successful life!

Now, let's get ready to do the work...

1

Rock Bottom

You don't find the cure to pain in a liquor store, or in a pint of ice cream. Believe me, I've tried. I've tried to find the cure to my pain in it all:

- Alcohol
- Food
- Men
- Fitness
- Gossiping
- Weight loss
- Binging

- Shopping

- Approval from others

- Toxic relationships

- Saying YES when I really wanted to say NO

- Trying to make others happy above my own happiness

If you're reading this list and thinking, "YEP! Check, check, check," you have picked up the right book. This book is a short story of how I went from rock bottom to real, authentic happiness. This book is about the work I did from the inside out, not the outside in, and how you can do it too.

My story is your story. It's everyone's story, because we are all suffering. We are all stopping ourselves in some way from being our best selves. I am not different from any of you reading this right now, but I am willing to be honest with myself and all of you *and* do the work. That is what has changed my life.

Are you ready to make a life change? And I mean a *real* life change. Not a don't-eat-carbs quick fix kind of change, but a change that will break toxic behaviors, toxic habits, and ultimately free you to be own your true self and live your full potential. If so, this book is for you.

We are going to the root of your issues. The real issues, the ones you've been avoiding, and everything you've been doing to numb yourself out. This book is about facing the root of your story, and why you think you are not good enough, smart enough, and worthy of success, love, and respect.

This book is about taking steps in a different direction. Changing your self-sabotaging, numbing out, addictive habits, and making a *real* sustainable change that will not only change your body, it will change your life!

I am going to take you through different stories in my life, then ask you to reflect on your own by answering questions at the end of each chapter and do your own work. You will find some chapters will be longer than others, but with every chapter, commit to the work. If you want true, long-lasting change and growth, you have to be willing to face what you have been trying to avoid for so long. And that takes work.

I'm going to start bold and open and tell you about one of my many addictions: alcohol. I know alcohol isn't everyone's issue, but we all have "something" that is our issue. It could be food, shopping, gambling, people-pleasing, etc. And whatever that something is, there is guilt and shame wrapped around it. My rock bottoms may be better or worse than your experiences, but they are my rock bottoms because it was at those moments that I hated myself. I was disappointed, disgusted, and ashamed of who I was. And, for me, that is what rock bottom means.

My dear friend alcohol. I've hit rock bottom many times, and in no particular order. Now, before you read on, keep in mind that I am a fitness professional. I am someone who tells people how to live a "healthy lifestyle," while at the same time I am an alcoholic who wouldn't admit it and someone who kept repeating the same toxic cycle over and over again. To say I was living a double life and being a total hypocrite would be an understatement. During all of these rock bottoms, I was a fitness trainer, kickboxing instructor, and mentor to many. Overall, I had everyone fooled, including myself.

Rock Bottom #1

It was another Monday that I called in "sick" or maybe I said I had an "emergency" and cancelled all my clients for the day. I was so hungover from Saturday night, which rolled into Sunday Funday brunch, that I felt the only thing that could make me feel better was another drink.

I would drink so much on the weekends that it wasn't just a hangover anymore. It was anxiety and depression. I called this the "alcohol blues." I would wake up with that feeling in the pit of my stomach the feeling of guilt, shame, embarrassment, and thoughts of "What did I say?" "What did I do?" and "Why do I keep drinking so much?"

That Monday started successfully enough. I got myself out of work and was on my way to my curing myself of shame and guilt by taking my first shot of vodka at 8am.

This was my life: lies, guilt, shame, and alcohol, and I was the best at it. The people I partied with over the weekend, who stopped to sober up on Monday, really did believe I was just sick. I was so good at coming up with excuses and stories, and the clients and co-workers I continued to let down and cancel on were the ones offering to help or bringing me soup when I was "sick." Or offering condolences when I said I got in a "car accident" to get out of work.

No one had a clue that this fun, successful fitness

girl had such a dark side. I'm not sure I even knew, or at least I don't remember. I don't remember when I went from a weekend party girl to the girl who drinks by herself or takes a shot at 8am. What I did know was, if at any point if I ever thought I was going to get found out, I would just elevate the lie even further. That way, I continued to get away with it. Even my own mother would text and call and ask if I was okay. I had everybody fooled, including myself. This is where my life got to and at that moment, I still didn't think I was an alcoholic or that I had a problem.

Rock Bottom #2

I ran the Boston Marathon. It was 2012 and I had signed up with my friend Megan to run for a charity. Her daughter has RETT syndrome and is in a wheelchair. We were running and raising money for her. We trained for months, raised over $5,000, and I felt ready until the week before the race.

My dad was very sick, and for me, my dad had always been a trigger. The news of his illness sent me into a bender. The last thing I remember was sitting on my couch, drinking vodka straight out of the bottle and trying to hide from the world, when my two friends knocked on my door. They somehow managed to pack my bag full of my running stuff, pour me into the car, and drive me from Santa Barbara to the Los Angeles airport where Megan and her daughter where waiting for me. I'm not even sure how I was allowed through security and onto the plane, but I was. Forty-eight hours later, I was at the start line of the Boston Marathon.

That year, it was record heat in Boston and people were passing out left and right on the course. Megan and I ran the whole thing side by side. When Megan would start to fade, I kept her going and vice versa. It wasn't until the last mile that I completely lost it. I had always thought to myself, "How could people run twenty-five miles and lose it in the last mile?" But there I was, recently sober enough to run a full marathon, and completely losing it in the last ten minutes.

I ran that last mile by myself with tears streaming down my face. I had so much anger and guilt and shame for all the lies and times I let everyone down. And so much confusion about who I was and how I was getting away with this double life. At that point, I looked up, saw the finish line, and literally did a cartwheel across it.

I had gotten away with it yet again.

Megan and me at the beginning of the Boston Marathon.

Rock Bottom #3

It was Christmas in Minnesota, and I could hear my niece and nephews screaming for me to wake up. I had promised to spend the entire day with them, starting early in the morning. I was so hungover I couldn't get

7

out of bed. I walked upstairs to find my sister fuming with disappointment, so pissed that I had broken another promise to her kids. I poured myself a coffee, found some Baileys Irish Cream liqueur, and suggested we all watch a movie.

My sister's judgmental looks and attitude brushed right off of me because, to be honest, I wasn't someone who took responsibility for her actions. Plus, I didn't have a problem. Coming home to Minnesota for the holidays was "my vacation," and I should've been able to party with my high school friends if I wanted to. My sister was the one with the problem. She had a stick up her ass. She was the one who wanted to get married and have kids, and then judged me for my lifestyle? "Screw her" was my attitude.

My sister and I barely spoke the rest of the holiday. At the same time, I couldn't look her kids in the eye because I had let them down. All they had wanted was to hang out with their aunt Jenny, and here I was angry at my sister for *my* actions.

Rock Bottom #4

My new boyfriend, who was a firefighter, had been gone most of the summer fighting fires. We had been acquaintances in the past and recently started dating after he asked if I could help get him in shape for fire season. He knew I liked to drink but assumed it was a social thing, and thought I was a blast to hang out with. He also really respected what I did as a fitness professional. He loved the fact that I was a female business owner who could control a crowd full of people with just my voice. He loved my drive, passion, and over-the-top energy. I never allowed him to see the dark side. I just kept painting the perfect picture of who I wanted him to think I was.

Until one day when he came over unannounced.

Connor walked into my apartment to find clothes all over the place, pizza boxes everywhere, and me completely passed out, sprawled across my bed with a bottle of vodka next to me. He stood there in utter shock. He had never seen anything like it, and he had never seen or imagined me this way passed out in the middle of the day on a random weekday. Is this what I did when he wasn't looking? The answer was yes. It's what I was doing when *everyone* wasn't looking.

Every addiction arises from an unconscious refusal to face and move through one's own pain. Every addiction starts with pain and ends with pain. Whatever the substance you are addicted to alcohol, food, legal or illegal drugs, a person you are using something or someone to cover up your pain. That is why, after the initial euphoria has passed, there is so much unhappiness and pain in addictions. They do not cause pain and unhappiness. They bring out the pain and unhappiness that is already in someone. Every addiction does it. Every addiction reaches a point where it does not work for you anymore, and then you feel the pain more intensely than ever.

I could end the book with that last paragraph. That is everything. I wish I could say that I wrote it, but I didn't. Eckhart Tolle did. But it spoke to me so clearly that I needed you to read it. And, I'll be honest, it is exactly what this book is about. It's about everything you have been avoiding, and everything you have been doing to numb yourself out. I know because I've been there. This is why most people don't change. They are unwilling to move through their own pain. So today, we are going to start with your biggest pain point.

THE WORK

1. **What is the one thing in your life that you know no longer serves you? What is your toxic anchor?**

   (You know what it is. You've felt this answer for a long time. It's always been in the pit of your stomach, or the back of your mind. For some of you, it is alcohol, for others it's food. Maybe it's needing approval. Be honest with yourself. No one is watching you and no one is judging you. This is the time to finally say it. Write down the ONE thing that you keep doing that brings you guilt and shame, and no longer serves you.)

2. Why do you think you do it?

(Is it a need to be happy, validated, or accepted? What part of your life feels unfulfilled?)

3. **Now sit with it for a minute. Write how it makes you feel to say it and acknowledge it.**

   (This is your moment to be honest with yourself. Let yourself just write. Do not hold back in any way. Write all the things that are coming up for you right now.)

The first step in my sobriety was admitting I was an alcoholic. The day I said it out loud, after fighting it for so long, was the day my entire life changed. This is step one, and it's not going to change overnight, but if you are willing to take this first step, TODAY, this is where the change begins.

2

Your Parents' Relationship

I grew up in what I thought was a pretty "normal" childhood. I am the youngest of three, and spent my childhood in the suburbs of Minnetonka, Minnesota. From the beginning, I was an outgoing kid full of energy and enthusiasm, always active and athletic. My mom says I was always smiling, dancing, and loud. She notes that I was born with a built-in microphone.

It's funny what you know as a kid without knowing it. For instance, think about your childhood. Think of the moments that we notice our parents not getting along but don't really understand how to process it. In our eyes, our moms and dads aren't really people with problems. They are just our parents. As a third grader, I didn't know about divorce. When I first heard what divorce meant, I blurted out, "My parents will get one of those."

My dad was the kind of guy who would leave work to take the "sales" guys out drinking for the afternoon and forget to pick me up from dance class. My mom was the kind of woman who did everything for our family. She always picked up after my dad and always seemed to make everything look good from the outside. I never knew exactly what was going on, but as a child I always felt a strange energy in our house, particularly between my parents.

I never remember my parents showing any affection, except for the one night I was supposed to be asleep and heard my dad begging my mom for something. I think it was their anniversary. I got out of bed and looked through the crack in their bedroom door to see my mom laying on her back lifeless, looking out into nothing, as my dad was on top of her. She looked miserable and bored.

My dad had a hard time showing affection. Everyone in my family really wanted it because it was so difficult to get. My mom, on the other hand, was the complete opposite. She has always been a ray of light, so full of love and attention. She would never let you leave her without a hug and kiss. I always felt warm and safe in her presence. I still do.

My mom was the glue that kept the things breaking in our family together. She was ALL the love, ALL of the affection. But looking back on it, she was also all of the facade. She did everything for everyone else. She put everyone else's happiness above her own, always. She never said no to anyone, even when she wanted to. She rarely spoke up for herself, and never talked about her own needs. She stayed in a marriage for twenty-three years, brutally unhappy because she didn't think she could make it on her own with three kids.

I want you to take a moment and think back to your childhood. Isn't it crazy what you realize now about your parents? We all now look back as adults and start to realize what was really going on.

Throughout this book, you are going to find that I am going to hit different trigger points from your life. Some will hit you, and some won't, but stay committed to doing the work. All of your answers will look different. Some of us have "daddy issues," and some of us have mom or sister issues or kid on the playground issues. Own your story, and go deep, because it's your unique story. Don't be ashamed to really look at it head on.

Before I met my husband, I was in one toxic relationship after another. What I realized from my childhood is that my mom was not happy, yet she made everyone think she was. In our family, you made the external world look good, and that's what it was all about.

I never realized, until a couple years ago, that as an adult, I always wanted my relationships to "look good." I wanted other girls to be jealous of what a great man I had because if I had what they wanted, it meant I was doing something right. I chased the popular, good-looking guy, the one who everyone wanted even if that meant he treated me horribly. As long as he appeared to be a "catch" to everyone else, that was all that mattered.

And to be honest, even if I did get the guy, I always felt the need to be desired by other men. That meant I would flirt and try to get away with what I could;

because if I was being desired by everyone around me, it also meant I was being accepted and loved.

I equated being **desired** with a (false) sense of **love** for a long time. And I now realize I was desperate to be loved and saved, just like my mom.

My brother Rob, Dad, Mom, Teri, and the baby is me

THE WORK

1. Now that you are an adult, what is it you realize about your parents' relationship when you were growing up? How does that make you feel?

2. Write about your own relationships. What toxic actions do you keep making? What toxic type of person do you keep seeking?

3. Is there a cycle you are repeating that you now realize was your parents' story/cycle?

3

Where Our Story Started

Now that I have you thinking about your family dynamics and childhood, let's keep it going.

We all have a moment in our childhood, usually between the ages of six and twelve, that shapes who we are today. My first pivotal moment was when I was six years old. I was all ready to go to my T-ball game, and my dad was the coach. I remember it like it was yesterday. I am standing at the bottom of the stairs as my mom is fixing my uniform. She's stressed because my dad is late, but still keeping the "everything's okay" smile on her face. Then I hear the garage door open and run upstairs to get my bag.

I stop at the top of the stairs to see my mom on the brink of tears and my dad so drunk he can barely stand. The next thing I know, I'm standing in the middle of them asking my dad why he can't come to my game, telling him I've been waiting for him, and it's time to go. He responds, "Your mother won't let me."

It was at that very moment that my dad shaped my life. I created the story that I, a six-year-old little girl, wasn't good enough for my dad to stay sober enough to make time for me. It was at that moment that my need for male attention, my need for acceptance, my need for validation from the outside world to feel good about who I am, was born.

We all have "that moment" that happened to us as a young child. It was either a parent, sibling, or a kid on the playground that did or said something that changed our story. I asked my mom to think back to when she was young, to whether anything like that ever happened to her.

My mom just turned seventy, and she was born and raised in the Midwest. It had been a long time since someone asked her to delve into her past. It took her a while, but one day she called me and said, "I was in fifth grade. I was standing in a circle of friends where I had just told a joke, and everyone was laughing until this one boy very loudly started making fun of me. Now everyone who had been laughing *with* me began laughing *at* me. It was at that moment I stopped speaking up. I became so scared of people thinking I was stupid that I just started trying to make everyone happy instead of speaking up. That way they wouldn't judge me."

My mom proceeded to tell me that she realized that, at that very moment, she created a story that her opinion didn't matter. That if she kept everything looking good on the outside and made people happy, no one would think she was stupid. She had been living out that same story since she was in fifth grade.

She stayed small, she stayed quiet, and she put what other people thought of her as a priority over her own happiness.

Can you relate to this? I know I can. I believe we all can.

My dad and me at my dance recital, age 6

THE WORK

1. **Take a minute and think about your "moment."**

   (You will know what the moment is because it will come to you clear as day, just like the example of my dad and me, or the kid on the playground for my mom. You will be brought right back to it. It's okay if it doesn't come right away. You may even have to come back to this. But when it does, write who it was, how old you were, and what they said.)

2. What story did you create out of that moment?

(An example of the story I created from my moment was that I wasn't good enough. And that if a man gives you his attention, you are worthy.)

3. **What limiting beliefs do you tell yourself over and over?**

    (Think about your self-talk. What do you say to yourself on a daily basis? For instance, "I am not good enough, smart enough, thin enough, I am not worthy of love…" What does that inner critic say?)

4

Peer Pressure

The first time I got drunk was the summer before ninth grade. My friend Kelly threw a party, and the tenth-grade boys showed up with alcohol. We thought we were so cool. Although I did not like the taste of beer, I found out quickly that I loved being drunk. I thought, "The faster I chug this, the less I taste it, and the better the feeling."

I will never forget when, in the middle of that party, one of the older boys handed me half of a beer and dared me to chug it. Of course, I answered his dare by showing off and chugging the beer. Then I realized the whole party was laughing at me. The boy shouted, "That is full of beer and chew spit, and Jenny just chugged it!" I was humiliated. Even my girlfriends were laughing.

I ran outside, puked, and then told myself that if I drank more, those hurtful feelings of shame and embarrassment would go away. I walked back into the party and told that tenth-grade boy to "F off," then opened a can of beer and chugged the whole thing. I was now invincible, and nothing could hurt me as long as I had this buzz going.

My need to be liked and accepted was both a high priority and huge insecurity for me. My freshman year of high school was brutal for me. I questioned everything: my body, my looks, my friends. I thought I wasn't as pretty, or as smart, or as cool as my friends, and overall, wasn't what boys looked for or liked in a girl. I began doing whatever I could to be noticed and fit in.

While writing this book, I found my high school diary. Here is my actual journal entry from May 10, 1995 (ninth grade):

I am so unhappy. I came home from school because I am depressed. Courtney, my best friend, is being a bitch. The guy I love likes someone else and I hate school, I hate everyone, I feel like no one likes me, and I want to switch schools. There are these older boys who call me "Butt", as in "butt ugly". Everyone thinks I am ugly. I feel like I can't be myself, I can't express my opinion to anyone because when I do, people make fun of me. All anyone does is drink and smoke weed on the weekends, and I hate it, but I do it to fit in. I've never done drugs, and last weekend someone gave me a sugar cube and I took it. I tripped out. Imagine me, a ninth grader, doing acid. I can't believe myself and I hate myself for doing it. I hate myself anyway, and everything about me. I am ugly and stupid. Why does it have to be like this? Sometimes I feel like I'm never going to stop crying.

I am now thirty-eight years old, and it is bizarre to read this journal entry and to write about these past experiences. I think, "Who was that little girl? How was I so lost and insecure, ruled by other people's opinions?"

The truth is, that was the story I had created way back when I was six years old. The day my dad came home too drunk to take me to T-ball. This story ruled my life and shaped my adolescence. I believed I wasn't good enough, and in order to be successful in life I had to be liked, desired, and popular. I had to make it all look good on the outside. Fitting in and being accepted was the only real goal.

Ninth grade with my best friend Courtney, who actually isn't a bitch and is still my best friend to this day.

THE WORK

1. **What was your first real low point, when do you can remember falling into peer pressure?**

    (Think about that first moment you did something that brought you shame and guilt something you knew wasn't right, but you did it anyway.)

2. Why did you do it?

3.   Write about how it feels to go back to that time.

5

Confronting Your Pain Person

Most of us have heard the term "daddy issues", right? Although I was always looking for male attention, and in need of structure, stability, and male guidance, I never thought of myself as someone who had "daddy issues."

Until I realized I was.

In order to grow, you have to go through the pain. So many of us try to go *over* the pain without working *through* the pain. Part of this can include facing the person who caused it, and a lot of us want to avoid doing that.

When I stopped drinking, I had to actually face

my issues head on without something to numb the true pain, and it wasn't easy. But it changed my entire life and my perspective. Especially about my father.

My dad grew up in a house with a verbally abusive mother and five siblings, all of whom were victims of her bouts of rage. His mother never showed affection, love, or praise for anything any of them did. They all grew up to be addicts in one way or another. One is a workaholic, one is a foodaholic, and the other four are alcoholics, although none of them would admit to any of it.

When I was growing up, my father was stiff and uncomfortable with my siblings and me. I never received a hug or a kiss from him that didn't seem awkward. We bonded through sports and, as I got older, alcohol and food. Yet, no matter what sport I played as a child, he would comment on how I could be better at a different sport. He would say things like, "Jennifer, great job on the tennis court, but you should play fast pitch like your sister." Then I would take his advice, and he would say, "Good job today at your softball game, but I bet you could swing a golf club." Nothing I ever did felt like enough. And, when you think about it, it makes sense because nothing he did growing up probably seemed good enough either.

My dad was an alcoholic, which is certainly something we had in common. I loved drinking with my dad because it was one of the only ways we connected. He was fun, loud, and the life of the party. People loved him when he was drunk. Despite this, I remember seeing an AA book on his dresser. Every January, he would quit drinking for a month to prove he didn't have a problem. I always knew he was struggling with an internal battle. In this way, we were very similar.

I remember the first time I confronted my dad and told him he wasn't there for me as a father; that he made me feel like I was never good enough. I had been drinking and was highly intoxicated. I was hoping for this huge, loving moment where he would say, "You're right Jennifer! I am so sorry, I love you so much, and I am so proud of you." Instead, he completely dismissed me and said, "Yeah Jennifer, we all know this. It's time for you to get over it and move on." I was heartbroken. I took it as, "This is how you handle hard situations. In order to be strong, you just move on."

The problem is, when you move on (or over it, as I like to say) without dealing with the actual issue, it shows up in different ways. Overeating, drinking too much, taking pills, shopping, gambling, people-pleasing. We try to numb out and avoid what we do not want to deal with.

In all honesty, it's never the actual addiction that's the problem. It's the story that was created long ago in childhood that is linked to all the things you don't want to deal with. This is the true problem.

It took me until I was sober and well into my thirties to realize *I wasn't living my OWN story; I was living my dad's story*. I was desperate for the approval of a man who didn't approve of himself. He was a child of verbal abuse who was constantly berated. He was never good enough for his mother and he always tried to prove himself. But inside, he felt like a failure. It was then I realized something important: how could I get love and approval from a man who didn't love and approve of himself?

We are so hungry for our parents' guidance, acceptance, and love, but we don't take into consideration how they were treated as children coupled with the ins and outs of their own family dynamic. I believe my parents (and your parents) did the best they could with what they had. For so many years, I was angry with my dad because I knew that, deep down, he had a huge heart, but he never let it show. He wanted to be affectionate toward his kids, but I later realized that he was never shown how to do that by his own parents. My father couldn't give me what I needed because he didn't know how.

Most of us are living out our parents' story. Oftentimes, we can't help it. It's all that we know. This shows the true power of a family cycle. I talked about this message in one of my classes how we often take on our parents' stories and issues. Later that day, I received an email from a client that said, "Jenny, after you shared your story today, I realized I always stand behind people in pictures. My mom hid behind people in every single picture because she had serious body issues. Today, I realized the significance of this, and now that I have a daughter, I must break this toxic cycle and face my body issues. This will happen NO MORE. My work starts now, and I will not pass this down to my daughter. The cycle ends here!"

When we stand up to the people that hurt us and choose to act from empathy for their story, our story changes. If we don't wake up to the toxic family cycle, it *will* continue. We have the power to change our lives, but we first have to undo everything that has been done.

My family cycle is alcoholism, food addiction, body issues, self-worth issues, and the belief that money makes you successful. I work every day to break these cycles so that I'm no longer held back by them, and most importantly, so that I don't pass them onto my own children.

My dad passed away at the age of sixty-five from Parkinson's, dementia, and ultimately, alcoholism. Before he passed, I went to his nursing home, played some Beach Boys, and fed him a hamburger. I told him how much I loved him and that I knew he did the best he could as a father. I forgave him, and I emphasized that he had to forgive himself. He needed to know he has three amazing and successful kids that love him. I told him I love my life, I love who I am, and I am grateful he was my dad.

I added one last statement. I leaned in and whispered in his ear, "Dad I quit drinking. I no longer need the approval of other people. I've realized I AM ENOUGH, and I know I am changing the dynamic of our family for the next generation." My dad had not moved in months, but at that moment, he squeezed my hand and smiled. The toxic family cycle we shared was broken.

This is where you get to change the story you have been telling yourself your entire life. Hopefully by now you have pinpointed the moment the story was created, and by who, and if you are willing it's time to give it back to that person. It's time to realize that it was their story, that it actually had nothing to do with you and everything to do with them. You just decided to take it on as your own. I know this because I took on my dad's story of never being good enough, of needing approval. That was all him. It never belonged to me. Now, I'm able to break the cycle, forgive, and move forward. I've made the choice to no longer continue with his story as my own. Now, I am on my own path accepting who I am, as I am, and I am okay with people who don't accept me. This is how you put an end to it; give the story back to who it belongs to.

My dad and me at my senior year Homecoming, 1998

The Work

1. Write a letter to the person who created your
    story.

2. **Think about their story and write about it.**

    (What do you know about THEIR childhood? How did they grow up, and how did their parents treat them?)

3. **Are you able to take a step back and see your childhood in a different way?**

   (*Is it possible for you to see your parents from a different perspective? Are you able to forgive? Are you able to give them their story back?*)

I would like to say, as a side note, that you may not be able to forgive and give back right away, and that is ok. You have been living with a huge weight, and it's going to take some time to allow the burden of that weight to be released. The more you do the work, the more you can start to unravel the truth about who you really are.

6

Food and Body Obsession

I believe that the way we do one thing is the way we do all things. My entire life, I've called myself an "extremist." I was an all-or-nothing kind of girl in everything I did. I was either blacked-out drunk or not drinking at all. I was either binging on "cheat" food or eating nothing but salads and smoothies. I was either lying on the couch all day watching TV or working twelve hours a day. Nothing in my life had balance.

This was especially true in when it came to the way I ate. In fact, eating for me looked more like dieting and binging. My family bonded over food in this way. My sister, mom, and I would all start together on Monday with the newest fad diet. One of us would suggest a diet that we heard worked for the neighbor or my sister's best friend or was the subject of the month's bestselling book, and we were convinced we had to try it. This would be the one that would finally change our bodies and make us all happy.

We would last about a week, then get together over the weekend and agree, as a team, that we were going to cheat. But we didn't just cheat, we binged. Sundays were known as the do-nothing cheat day. We would literally sit around and eat everything we were not supposed to eat, which meant Chinese food for lunch, pizza for dinner, and sandwiches and chips in between. All of this occurred while sitting on the couch watching Lifetime movies. Sounds kind of amazing, doesn't it?

As I write this, I actually get a warm feeling over my body thinking about the Sundays with my sister and mom. The problem was that they became a replacement for talking about real issues happening in our lives. Instead, we focused on what we were eating (or not eating) or what we were going to do to lose weight. It was a constant conversation in our house, and I chalked it up as normal, when what I was really doing was setting the stage for many of my food issues.

Drinking was the most obvious extreme habit I had, but it wasn't the only one. Food was another big one. Because I wasn't throwing up (bulimia) or not eating (anorexia), I didn't think I had an eating disorder. I thought it was normal to constantly diet and have cheat days and obsess about food, because it's what my family did. Although I was always jealous of my friends who didn't seem to have food issues. You know the ones who can just eat whatever they want and stop when they're full like it's not a big deal, the ones who don't obsess about what they eat. I always wanted to be one of those people.

I didn't really realize this until my second most influential childhood story, which came to me in the most unconventional way. A couple of years ago, I was in Palm Springs, California, and I met a breathing coach named Bill. I know what you're thinking, because I was thinking the same thing: "Seriously a breathing coach? Give me a break." But, at this point in my life, I was on a quest of self-care and willing to try anything, so I booked a session with him. When he asked what I wanted to work on, I told him I had no control over food. I shared that I was constantly binging and dieting, obsessed about my weight and the way my body looked, and that I compared my body to everyone around me.

He had me do the most bizarre breathing technique that put me into a trance. He started asking me questions, and guess what? Out came my childhood food story. It wasn't just the binging and dieting with my mom and sister. It got deeper and led into the time when my mom went back to work to help save my dad's business. I was left home alone after school and most of the evening. My parents were at work, my siblings were older, and the last thing my brother and sister wanted was to hang out with their little sister. I was scared and lonely, so I would turn on all the TVs in the house, get a bunch of food, set it all out on the table, and binge while watching TV. Eating was my coping mechanism for feeling abandoned, lonely, and scared. At ten years old, food equaled comfort and love. I realized at thirty-seven years old that I was still using that same coping mechanism.

For twenty-five years of my life, I used food much

like alcohol to help me escape. Anytime I felt overwhelmed, sad, or frustrated, I would get a smorgasbord of food, watch TV, and binge. It was another way of numbing out. I would tell myself it was just part of my extreme energy and attitude, that "all or nothing" was just who I was. I would also justify it, just as I justified alcohol, saying, "I earned this. I work hard. I get to treat myself." The other story I constantly told myself was that I was just a big eater, that I had no control over food, and the only way I could lose weight was to diet and restrict what I ate.

The food obsession only contributed to my body image obsession, which contributed to my self-worth obsession. And here is the problem with all of that: for most of us, even when we are at our "goal weight," we don't even know it because we are so obsessed with what still needs to change. We're saying to ourselves, "Well, I could lose a couple more pounds; my arms still aren't toned enough. If I just cut a little more out of my diet, then it will work, and I will be happy." It's never enough.

I learned that the issue wasn't with food. The issue was with my *relationship* with food and what I ultimately used food for. It was a coping mechanism, and it worked for my ten-year-old self but no longer worked for my thirty-seven-year-old self.

This is what I mean when I say that no matter what you're struggling with alcohol, food, pills, needing constant attention, people-pleasing it all leads us to the same finish line: *an unfulfilled life*. And that is how you know it's a toxic anchor. It's the action of repeating a toxic behavior/cycle that brings guilt and shame to numb yourself out and not feel good about yourself.

After I met with Bill the Breathing Coach, I stopped blaming my toxic behaviors as being part of my extremist personality or "just how my family is" or declaring that I earned it. I realized this all came from a deep-rooted part of my childhood and feeling abandoned. And, that what served me to cope as a ten-year-old no longer worked. You know what? That's when I was able to finally change my relationship with food.

THE WORK

1. **What toxic behavior do you keep repeating that you tell yourself is "just part of your personality" or "just who you are," yet you know it doesn't serve you?**

   (For instance, mine was constant dieting and binging telling myself I was just a big eater when in fact I had no control over food.)

2. When did you first start having the issue? How old were you?

3. Write down that this it is NOT "just part of who you are." You choose who you are.

7

Adult Peer Pressure

During my senior year of high school, I got accepted to the University of Minnesota. I always had a gut feeling that I needed to get out of Minnesota, so I applied to a couple of schools out of state. My parents never really pushed me toward college, and my grades were not great. I guess I never really took it that seriously until it came down to that "Oh sh*t" moment when everyone was asking me where I was going to college.

The University of Minnesota was where everyone from my high school was going. I already had my dorm. I was basically in my sister's sorority since I was a legacy, and I accepted that as my fate. I would do everything I was "supposed to do" after high school: go to college, join a sorority, get a job, a husband, have kids, and live in Minnesota for the rest of my life.

I was sitting in class a month before school got out when an acquaintance asked, "What are you doing next year?" I told her I was going to the U of M, just like everyone else, and she said, "I am going to California and I need a roommate."

I had never had an *aha* moment in my life, one of those moments where you feel it to your core. This was one of them. I felt like she was placed next to me at that exact moment or that a higher power had sent her to me to tell me this was really my fate. I went home that day and said to my mom, "I have the opportunity to go to California and I think I should go." My mom looked at me and to my surprise, without even hesitating she said, "GO! I think you should really GO!"

One month later, I packed my Chevy Blazer and hit the road with my high school boyfriend, who planned to drive me out there and drop me off. I had never been to California. In fact, I had barely even left the state of Minnesota. Taylor, the girl who got me to make the move, had an apartment set up in San Diego, close to San Diego State University. That first week was exhilarating and scary, and I couldn't wait to start my new life.

I quickly realized I did not fit in at all. I was a tomboy with short hair, and all the girls wore miniskirts to the grocery store. Girls were not as friendly as they were in Minnesota, and people didn't go out of their way to meet new people, especially if you weren't in their dorm or sorority.

I enrolled at the local junior college and joined the dance club in hopes of meeting new people. I ended up meeting some great people who lived in our apartment complex, but I found that with a new beginning and a new start, the insecurities inside of me only became more pronounced. I was insecure, out of place, didn't feel pretty enough or girly enough, and didn't own a miniskirt! I was lost, terrified, and I felt alone in a new state. It felt like freshman year of high school all over again.

Everything was scary for me, from driving on the freeway to trying to meet new friends. I had no idea how to talk or act around people, so I drank, ate, and tried to be cool by doing what I could to fit in. I remember one night going to a party and finding out what the drug "ecstasy" was. I took it because that was what everyone else was doing. I wanted desperately to fit in. While everyone else was all touchy feely and dancing around, I was huddled in a corner, feeling awful and having an incredibly bad experience.

They say that if you go into drugs with a bad mindset, you'll have a bad trip. Maybe this is why I liked drinking so much. When I drank too much, I would either just black out, pass out, or order a pizza. Drugs were a different story for me. Once you took them, you couldn't get out of them. But, just like when I was in ninth grade, I fell into peer pressure and took drugs because I was desperate to be accepted. It sounds like a *Sweet Valley High* book or an after school special, but peer pressure is very real, and even as adults, we fall into it.

Think about it. Have you ever gone out with friends and they gave you a hard time because you weren't drinking? Or, has anyone ever given you a hard time about working out, or choosing to do something that makes you feel good? It usually goes like this: "Oh you're so lame. You're not drinking tonight? Come on, loosen up, you deserve it! Have some fun." Even when masked with sarcasm, these things can actually change the way we make decisions.

I remember trying to quit drinking as an adult (for the millionth time) and going out with a friend or acquaintance who would make me feel embarrassed for not having a drink. After a little rousing from friends, I would eventually give in and talk myself into having a drink. Because I wasn't feeling strong enough in who I was, I let other people's opinions dictate my own. It wasn't until I looked at my pain and addictions that I realized it was up to me to make the shift, no matter what anyone thought. And truly, what does me NOT drinking have anything to do with how someone else's night turns out?

It can happen with anything you're trying to do or not do. There will always be people who will say something negative or discouraging about it. Some people feel guilty about their own lives or don't want other people to succeed and be happy because they are unhappy. If you're usually the most intoxicated one at the party and, all of a sudden, you're not drunk, where does that leave them? People who give you a hard time about making positive choices in your own life usually reflects the fact that they are in a dark place, and they don't want to see you go to the light. They may not even realize it, but their criticism about your positive choices actually has nothing to do with you and everything to do with them. The problem is, if you're not strong and healthy about yourself, you're going to fall into it.

THE WORK

1. I want you to think of one significant peer pressure moment from when you were young and spend a few minutes writing about it.

2. Now, think of a time as an adult where you faced peer pressure and write about it below.

3. Finally, write what you are going to do the next time you find yourself in a peer pressure moment.

8

Abusive Boyfriend

The girls I had become friends with from my apartment complex in San Diego were going to Santa Barbara for the weekend and invited me to go with them. This was before Facebook or Instagram, but someone told me there were two girls who graduated a year ahead of me from Minnetonka that now lived in Santa Barbara. I knew who they were, so I found their phone numbers and decided to give them a call. I said I was coming to Santa Barbara for the weekend, and they welcomed me with open arms.

It only took one weekend in Santa Barbara and I was in love with the town! Isla Vista was the greatest place I had literally ever been to. It's the college town for University of California Santa Barbara (UCSB) and one full of young people who party. I felt like I had found my own personal Disneyland. Picture a town full of kids right at the edge of the ocean, where everyone just walks from party to party, drinking all day! Some people went to UCSB and some went to Santa Barbara City College, but more importantly, the main focus of this town was to get your party on. Needless to say, I WAS HOME!

At the end of the weekend, Sonia and Katie (my new friends who I had known vaguely in high school) told me they'd have an open room in their place starting the next school year. Once again, I went home and proclaimed, "I am moving to Santa Barbara." Sure enough, a couple of months later, I left San Diego to head north.

Santa Barbara (or "SB," as we like to call it) was my jam. I *loved* it. I loved Katie and Sonia and all the amazing, crazy people I met there. It was a cool beach town where people were nice to each other. Doors were always open, people were always down to party, and I fell head over heels in love. I felt like I finally had a close-knit group of girlfriends who all looked out for each other and partied together.

I met my first college boyfriend, Dominic, in Isla Vista, a town near Santa Barbara. He was the life of the party. He was incredibly intelligent but partied like a wild man. I will never forget the night I went to a Halloween party at his house, dressed like a cowgirl. He came over to talk to me, and I felt like my whole world had just opened up. Everyone knew Dom, and here he was, talking to *me*. He was more than just talking to me, he was hitting on me, and it made me feel so special!

I dated Dom on and off for years. He was one of the first guys to open me up to my sexuality. I was very insecure about my body, and although I had had sex before him, I'm never sure I really enjoyed it. Dom was an academic but also a free spirit, and he was so open and encouraging about being free with your body. He taught me that sexuality is confidence and how to own it and love it. This was one of the first times I remember feeling sexy, powerful, and confident in my own skin.

Dom was a force even at twenty-something years old. He had this charismatic energy and attitude, not to mention the fact that he was so smart. But the truth about Dom was that he was also a raging alcoholic, and our fantasyland relationship quickly turned toxic. He knew I was insecure and fed off of it. If he didn't get his way and was blacked-out drunk, he had no problem throwing me around. He was the king of getting wasted, cheating on me, or having a knock-down-drag-out fight with me, which usually ended with holes in the wall or bruises on my body. He would then be able to turn it all around the next day, buy me something, or do something outlandishly sweet, and I would take him back. This lasted way longer than it should have, but being an insecure alcoholic myself, I stayed in it thinking this was normal or "not that bad." Everyone loved Dom and Dom loved me, so that made me special.

Never in a million years did I think that I would be in an abusive relationship. I was the girl who would ask, "How could anyone ever allow a man to treat her that way?" But here I was, that girl. It wasn't until Dom slept with my best friend and roommate and threw me across the room in front of everyone that I finally said, "Enough."

Looking back, I stayed with Dom because I felt

65

acceptance from other people when I was with him. It tied back to many of the stories I've shared about my childhood in this book. He was popular and always had a lot of attention from people, so therefore *I* always had a lot of attention on me. It played into all of my own toxic issues.

This is the problem with looking for our own validation from other people. We end up making decisions based on what other people think. For instance, everyone thought Dom was great. Even though I knew better, other people liked him and would tell me how lucky I was, so I convinced myself they were right.

Toxic relationships aren't only possible with the people we date or marry. We can have them with family, friends, coworkers, and just about anybody else in our lives. When you love who you are, you don't hurt other people, and you don't allow people to hurt you. I guess you could say Dom was just as insecure as I was. He just faked it better. It took a long time for me to realize that I was enough without him.

THE WORK

1. Think of a toxic love relationship you were in or ARE in. Think about how old you are, how you feel about yourself, and why you stay in the relationship. Set a timer for five minutes and write all the feelings that come up right now.

2. Dig a little deeper and ask yourself what underlying reason or issue might be causing you to have stayed, or continue to stay, in your toxic relationship.

3. How did you break free of it, or how can you break free from it if you're still in it?

9

Finding My Career

I still loved Santa Barbara, and I wasn't going any-
where. I have always loved working out, but I
couldn't afford a gym membership. So I applied for
a job at the local Gold's Gym, working the front desk.
I was twenty years old, and I still wasn't sure what I
wanted to do with my life.

As an employee of the gym, I was allowed to
workout for free and take all the classes I wanted, so
I immersed myself in the culture of this small-town
gym. I was immediately drawn to a woman named
Chanda. She was the group fitness director and the
most amazing, fit, confident woman I had ever met.
She was everything that I wasn't, and I wanted to be
her. I went to every class she taught, all of which were
jam-packed with people waiting in line to get a spot.

She walked around with an energy about her, as if she knew who she was and didn't care what you thought of her. All at the same time, her charisma could control an entire room as well as her words, movement, and energy.

One day after a cardio kickboxing class, Chanda asked me if I ever thought about teaching. She said, "You have rhythm, people seem to like you, and you're LOUD! I think you would make a great teacher. Let me teach you how to teach." My initial reaction was, "No way." There was no way I could do what this incredible woman was doing. I didn't have her confidence, her body, her draw. No way, no how. I couldn't do it, so I said no.

After a couple days of pestering, Chanda convinced me to at least train with her, and she soon became my mentor. We trained for months, and during that time she taught me how to cue music, choose beats, count, kick, and strategies for when you get tired on stage. I also learned how to break down combinations, structure a class, and stretch. She even gave me weekly quizzes, which I hated because I never wanted to disappoint her.

All of this training behind the scenes led me to the moment I finally taught my own class. We broke it up so that Chanda would teach the first half, and I would teach the last twenty minutes or so. Within the first five minutes of me taking over and teaching her class, people started walking out of the room. I was devastated. I had failed. People didn't like me. I wasn't Chanda, and therefore, I wasn't good enough.

I told Chanda I couldn't do what she did. But the funny thing was, for the first time in my life, I kept showing up. I kept training. I kept teaching, and guess what? People kept walking out of my class.

One day Chanda brought me the comment box and said, "All of these have your name on them" and started to read them out loud to me:

"Jenny's too loud."

"Jenny's music is too loud."

"Why is Jenny teaching Chanda's classes?"

"When is Chanda coming back?"

"Jenny's too loud, Jenny's too loud, Jenny's too loud."

I looked at her with tears in my eyes and said, "Why would you read these to me? Are you trying to break me? Are you trying to get me to quit? Because if you are, I am there."

At that moment, Chanda looked at me and said, "Do you have a passion for this? Do you love people and music and movement? Not everyone is going to like you, but DO YOU LIKE YOU?"

At that moment, my life took a turn. Up until that point, I had never been asked if I liked myself. It stopped me in my tracks. Chanda said that I had to stop trying to be her, stop trying to please everyone, and start being myself. My true, authentic self. She also wisely informed me that the people who are drawn to me were supposed to be, and the people who weren't...well...those just weren't my people.

From that moment on, I embraced my loudness. I started teaching classes on my terms, with my own music and my own moves. And, in only a month, my classes were like a VIP night club. You had to wait in line to get in, and night after night the room was packed!

What's funny is that the very things about myself that I often felt uncomfortable or insecure about (my body, my loudness) were the things that made me a great fitness class instructor.

THE WORK

1. Do you like YOU?

2. Whether you answered yes or no, WHY?

3. What is one thing about yourself that sets you
   apart from other people?

10

You Can't Change for Other People

My classes had become so popular that the manager of Gold's gym suggested I become a personal trainer. His name was Mike, and he was like a father figure to me. I worked at Gold's Gym for almost seven years and met my incredible mentor (Chanda) during that time. At one point, I went to Mike and told him I wanted to start my own business. He told me he didn't think I was ready yet, that I was too irresponsible. To this day, I still believe he had my best interests in mind. Yes, I'm sure he didn't want to lose an employee, but he was teaching me a lesson. Because when I came back to him a year later and said, "I have an opportunity to become an independent contractor and start my own business at a small boutique gym," he said, "Go. You're ready!"

Although I had matured, felt ready to move on, and believed I had changed, there were still some very toxic behaviors that had not. I had made a name for myself in Santa Barbara. People were asking my advice on how to live and be healthy. I was becoming the fitness expert. But I was also living a double life, and I was really good at living both.

As my career was advancing, so were my toxic behaviors. Every week I worked hard. Up at 5am, home at 9pm, and as passionate as ever about fitness. Here I was, guiding people and telling them daily how to live better, eat better, and move better, all while drinking more, getting more and more drunk every weekend, and engaging in all sorts of other unhealthy things. It was still all or nothing. I was preaching one thing and doing the complete opposite.

Oftentimes we think, "If only I had more money," or "If I could just lose these last ten pounds," or "If I just found the right partner," or "If only I had a better job/house/car," everything would be different. Here's the truth: you can lose all the weight in the world, but if you don't like the person you see in the mirror, your life will never change. You can have the "perfect" man walk into your life, but if you don't love yourself first, he will never fully be able to give you all that you need. You can redecorate your house, buy all the fancy purses, cars, and clothes you want, but the outside will never look good enough if you are not healthy and whole on the inside.

My job, life, and friends completely exceeded anything I could have imagined the day I left Minnesota for California after high school. I thought I'd end up going to the University of Minnesota, getting married, and having kids. And here I was, in the most amazing city, Santa Barbara, doing what I loved for a living, with a great group of friends, coworkers, and mentors around me. But it did not change who I was on the inside, and that person was an insecure, people-pleaser who used alcohol and food to numb out and escape from life. I am living proof that you can have the "perfect" life or work you love, and it won't change who you are inside. Because, underneath it all, I was struggling with my core issue of not feeling good enough.

Life is a lot like a new diet. Many of us are looking for the external thing that will help us change our lives. We think this or that will do it for us, and we'll finally feel happy and fulfilled. But what really happens is, we all try the diet and it lasts about a week. Then we fall back into our old patterns and behaviors, feel guilty, and start the whole process all over again. The problem is we are seeking the quick fix instead of identifying the root of the problem.

The only real way we can change our lives is by starting from within. But we don't want to go back and think about what created the actual problem in the first place. How often do we ask ourselves, "Why do I overeat?" "Why do I continue to drink so much?" "Why do I shop" "Why do I put others' happiness above my own?" We are so quick to tell ourselves it's because we don't have the willpower or we are weak, when that is actually not the case. Asking these tough questions and really getting the true answers would really mean sifting through our past and healing. It is not easy, and that's why a lot of people don't do it.

I did this for a really long time myself. How did I have all I wanted, but still go home at night and on the weekends, get drunk, eat everything in the kitchen, and always wake up with guilt and shame? What finally happened to me is what happens to a lot of people: my issues got bigger and more painful until they became harder to hide and escape, and that was when I finally realized I had change from within first.

It is easy to disregard *why* we created our unhealthy habits and where they came from. It's possible to understand our patterns in order to change them. Instead, we often try to skip over the hard part and attempt to use our own willpower to change. Or, we think that we'll be who and what we want once we have what we want. That's why it doesn't last! And that is why the toxic cycle continues and is passed on for generations to come.

I want you to know that you don't lack willpower and you are not weak. You have the ability to break the cycle, and if you are still reading this book, you are doing that. I am proud of you.

THE WORK

1. **Are you relying on any outside issues to make the changes you want in your life? If so, what are they?**

    (For instance, "Once I find love, once I make more money, once I can drive this car...")

2. **What issues within yourself might be the root of the problem instead?**

(Mine, for example, was never being good enough. That's why all the exterior stuff was never enough.)

3. **Write down one thing you can do to change your perspective.**

   (Mine was realizing that true happiness comes from how I feel about myself in the present. Every day I stick a Post-It on the mirror that says, "I am Enough.")

11

Double Life

'll be honest, I'm a really good bullshitter.

I could always talk my way back into people's good graces. My mom was a bit of an enabling mother, so I rarely got in trouble. I learned at a young age that if I pissed people off, I could always find a way to get them back. I would tell little lies, turn on the charm, and could talk my way out of anything.

I was the kind of person who had party FOMO, "fear of missing out", and that would take priority over everything. I would cancel or get substitute teachers for my classes because I didn't want to miss going to the bars, or to a house party on a Friday night. I would call in sick or cancel personal training clients with some B.S. excuse because I was so hungover that I couldn't leave my apartment. Despite all of this, I was always able to win people back and rarely lost clients.

At this point in my life story, I was an entrepreneur working for myself and still maintaining my double life. I had taken a job as an independent contractor, training out of a boutique personal training gym. The gym's owner, Mike, soon became another mentor to me. He introduced me to the "who's who" of town, which included Kathy Ireland. Kathy soon became one of my clients. Kathy is a supermodel-turned-businesswoman and an overall incredible human. Even with her celebrity status, she took the time to get to know me and saw my talent as well as noticed my troubles. I would show up to our 5:30am training sessions hungover, and although she never said anything about it, one day she handed me a book.

I am not very religious, or I should say, I believe in God, but I struggle with organized religion and the hypocrisy that can come with it. Kathy Ireland is probably the most Christian woman I know, and she truly lives her life authentically for God. She definitely walks the walk. She doesn't gossip about people, she's not a hypocrite, and her family is very close-knit, loving, caring, and puts God first.

I will never forget the morning she gave me a Bible with this written to me inside the cover:

Jenny,

May the Lord Jesus continue to bless, guide, and protect you. May you always know and feel His unconditional love for you. Keep your eyes on Him and He will carry you through every storm. May you be filled with His holy spirit, His perfect peace, and His love.

God Bless you,
Kathy

It's funny what we think we are getting away with, what we think other people don't know or notice, and how we are oblivious to the fact that they do, in fact, know. The moment after Kathy gave me that Bible, I realized that my stories were, in fact, getting old. People were talking about me. I was quickly becoming the flaky trainer people couldn't rely on. I thought the lies I was telling and the facade I was creating were working! Maybe they had at one time, but not anymore.

We are all addicts in some way or another, and there is a dark side to ourselves that we all try to hide from everyone else. Some people say they buy all their shopping purchases on sale to hide their shopping addiction. Others lie and say they "can't lose weight" because they were just born with that body, when in reality they are binge eating every night after work. Some, like myself, claim that they don't have a real problem with alcohol because they are a functioning human with a job and their own apartment. In reality, they're living in complete chaos, guilt, and shame.

Rather than admit we have a problem, we make up stories and excuses. I know because I was one of the best at it! The reality is, we usually aren't fooling people. Or, we can only do so for a while before they start to notice.

It would still be awhile before I got sober, but I

will say that the Bible was another *aha* moment that made me realize I wasn't as good of a bullshitter as I thought and that, quite possibly, people were starting to see through the facade. Today, I don't just tell the truth, I *own* my truth. And, let me tell you, it's a lot better than trying to lie and cover up my tracks.

Kathy Ireland and me at my wedding

I used to be so ashamed of my past that I would never bring it up. It wasn't until I told my husband all of my dirty little secrets that the guilt and shame were lifted. I'm not saying you have to sit your family down and tell them every horrible thing you've done. And, just FYI, we all have our own secrets. I believe the moment we say it, write it, and acknowledge that it happened, we make the choice to move forward. It starts with being honest to yourself, to your family, to your friends, and to everybody else. If you don't feel comfortable saying it, write it down to acknowledge it and share it later. Your past is not your life sentence. Be honest about it so you can release it and move on.

The Work

1. Write three times you told lies in your life and got away with it. They can be big or small. Even if you have never ever admitted them before, write them out.

2. Write about what kind of feelings it brings up when writing about the lies.

3. **If you were to tell the truth from this point forward, what do you think would happen?**

12

The Man Who Changed My Life

I have always been afraid of who I really was. When I drank, I didn't care what people thought, and that was freedom. I had a huge fear of failure and rejection, and I never thought I was worthy of success. I would self-sabotage a lot. Any time things were going well for me, I would screw it up. I was so scared of who I was and my own true potential and success, I would subconsciously ruin relationships and opportunities, both personal and professional. Drinking let me be wild and free without any apology, explanation, or a care as to what anyone else thought.

It also allowed me to hide from my true potential.

I thrive off of the attention of groups, energy, people, and community. That's my jam. I *loved* teaching because my classes were LOUD and packed with students. People would shout and cheer, and I loved every minute of it. At that time, Gold's Gym had changed its name to Spectrum. I kept all of my personal training clients at the private boutique gym during the day and continued teaching group classes at night at Spectrum. Those classes continued to be as popular as ever.

This is how I met the man who would ultimately help change my life and become my business partner. At forty-seven years old, Stephen Stowe had never been to a gym. The story he tells is that he was in a very toxic relationship and did not want to go home after work, so he joined the local gym. His perspective on gyms was that everyone was working out, but no one was ever talking to one another. Everyone either had their headphones on while TV or was looking in the mirror, taking selfies. What he saw was a potential for a community, as so many people were there for the same reason: to improve their lives in one way or another. Yet no one was connected.

Stephen found the gym intimidating, as he had no idea where to start or what to do, so he walked back downstairs and saw a line outside of the group fitness room. He asked the front desk what was going on and they told him, "Oh that's Jenny's cardio kickboxing class! It's the most popular class at the gym." Needless to say, he took a chance and tried my class. That very day, both of our lives changed.

It was during that class that Stephen saw my talent to command a room, my full-blown energy, and my ability for bringing a room together through movement. After coming to class for a couple weeks, he walked up, introduced himself, and said to me, "If you ever want to take this to the next level, I can help you."

At that moment I thought, "Who is this weirdo and what does he want from me?!" I immediately questioned what he wanted from me, or whether it was some kind of creepy pick-up line, so I just smiled and said, "Oh thank you" and totally blew him off.

Even though I completely dismissed him and he knew it he kept coming back to class. It wasn't until a couple of months later that he approached me again. This time, he handed me an article about "The Oprah Effect." It said that when Oprah talks about something, it catches on like wildfire. Stephen said to me, "I could get you here." At that moment, I figured, "What do I have to lose?" and we began a friendship.

It was six months into our business relationship and friendship that he noticed I took drinking to the extreme. We had been out on more than one occasion, and I remember him saying to me, "It's like you just can't have one or two, you always take it to the extreme. Maybe this is a problem." He challenged me to go six months without drinking. I really respected Stephen, and I wanted him to respect me, so we shook hands and agreed that when I turned thirty, on December 29th, I would quit drinking for six months.

My friends and family could not believe it. People even commented that there was no way I would make it six months without alcohol. I'll be honest, I wasn't sure if I could make it either. I had never in my life had gone that long without drinking. I wanted to prove to Stephen that I could do it, and I succeeded.

In those six months, our business took off. I was

laser-focused on my work, working out, and what I ate. I was like a hermit. If I wasn't at work, I was at home or working out. I didn't know what to do with myself, because all I knew besides work was partying with my friends. I didn't trust myself to go out, so I just stayed in and stayed clear of all temptation. I lost twenty pounds and was physically in the best shape of my life.

But, while I physically looked in the best shape of my life, I was still a mess on the inside. I was still obsessed with how I looked, thinking it was never good enough. I would look in the mirror and tell myself that my stomach could still be flatter, my thighs were still too big, and I needed to define my arms more. I was getting noticed more, and more people were signing up for the bootcamp program I had created. Although it all looked successful on the outside, I was internally very unhappy. I questioned everything I did and whether people liked me and approved of what I was doing. I was living in a constant state of "It's never good enough," and I was miserable.

The moment the six months was up, can you guess the first thing I did? Yep, I drank. I thought that going six months without drinking meant that I didn't really have a problem, so I could go ahead and start drinking again. After those "successful" six months, for the next three years of my life my drinking became worse! Why? Because: YOU CANNOT CHANGE FOR SOMEONE ELSE. IT WILL NOT LAST.

What I learned from those six months, which I would not realize until later, is that you cannot change for other people. Real, long-term change only happens when you truly want it for yourself; when you are sick and tired of being sick and tired. When you've had enough of your own B.S. toxic story. That is when change happens.

Stephen Stowe and me

THE WORK

1. **Have you ever made a promise and made a change for someone else?**

   (For example, "I will lose ten pounds for you" or "I will give up ___ for you" or "I will change careers for you.")

2. Did it last? If not, why?

3.   If it did, what changed in you?

13

Nobody's Perfect

At this point in my story, I was thirty-two years old and a full-blown alcoholic. After not drinking for six months, I felt totally lost. I had no idea who I was because I was still making decisions to please people and look good to others instead of looking inside of myself. I didn't quit drinking for myself; I quit for someone else. I was sick of living the toxic cycle of trying to constantly prove myself to other people.

Ironically, as I mentioned in the previous chapter, it was after those six months of being sober that my drinking actually got worse and began taking on a life of its own. And, to be brutally honest, I was sleeping around, drinking by myself, lying to others, and making horrible decisions. I had come to my darkest place yet.

I would come up with crazy stories, like I fell and got a concussion, so that I didn't have to go to work so that I could stay home and drink. My excuses started to become bigger and more outrageous. I would look people straight in the eye and lie without even flinching. People actually had sympathy for me because they believed whatever story I told them. I even had people sending me flowers. At the same time, I was hiding inside my apartment, drinking a bottle of vodka all by myself. I was so good at this double life that when I did finally admit I was an alcoholic, a lot of people didn't believe me!

I don't know what it is about vodka in particular, but I never drank it until I became a full-blown alcoholic. It's the alcoholic's "drink of choice." It doesn't smell, it's clear, and it's easy to hide. While bizarre, I drank vodka for a long time and nobody knew, including my friends and family. In all honesty, there were points where I would have a drink and go to work. No one noticed.

I was lying and covering up my problem so that I could keep drinking. I was also afraid of admitting I had a problem. I didn't want to be that person who has issues, the one who didn't have it all together. I wanted to keep my facade going the façade that I was this great, accomplished trainer and successful businesswoman. Which I was. Except, I was also an alcoholic.

It can become so important to present the image we want others to see. We will increasingly go to extremes to do it. How many times have you hidden the fact that you don't have the perfect marriage? Or you can't stand your kids sometimes? Or you struggle with insecurities or body issues?

It was the fear of not being enough, not being perfect, not being liked or not fitting in that, in part, drove my drinking in the first place. Way back when I was in ninth grade and felt horrible about myself, alcohol helped me overcome it. I didn't want to be imperfect, so I hid behind drinking.

It wasn't until I began admitting that I had an issue that I realized that other people aren't perfect either. That we are all struggling with something. Every time I share that I am struggling with in my life or my work, there is at least one other person who tells me he or she is struggling also.

I am here to tell you that nobody is perfect, and that includes you. But I am also here to remind you that most people are not expecting you to be. The more you are open and honest about your story and your struggles, the more you will find you are not alone.

THE WORK

1. Do you struggle with perfectionism or a fear of not being perfect? If so, in what way?

2. Do you think people expect you to be perfect?
   If so, who and how?

3. What would happen if you admitted you were
    not perfect and that you had issues, to yourself
    or others?

14

Acknowledging the Problem

A ddiction is a progressive disease. When an addict stops for a little while, a lot of times it works for a short period. I would get to the point where I would stop drinking for a week or two, maybe even a month, and feel so clear and confident. I truly thought I could drink "casually" or in moderation and handle it. I would have a couple of positive experiences drinking, like maybe only having two glasses of wine instead of a bottle, or not blacking out. I chalked that up as having control. But this never lasted long, and eventually I would be back to blacked-out and the guilt and shame spiral that came with it.

I was caught in the cycle a million times over, but on October 11th, 2012, something changed.

I thought "rock bottom" would be one big blow that would change my life completely, but as I shared earlier in my story, I hit a bunch of rock bottoms. The way I came to stop drinking altogether was through another life-changing *aha* moment.

I was attending a seminar with one of my favorite trainers, Todd Durkin. He was talking about how so many people, especially fitness trainers, live double lives. He said, "In the training world, trainers will tell people how to exercise, eat, and live a healthy life, yet they are the ones out every night over drinking and overeating." Then he spoke a quote that literally changed my life: **"In order to be a leader, you must be the example."**

On that day, it was like my pen just took over, and on the edge of the notebook on which I was taking notes, I wrote:

"10-11-12 I am an alcoholic and I will not drink again."

It was the first time I admitted I was an alcoholic, first to myself, and then to my business partner. It was something I'd never before said but had known my entire life. I'd avoided saying it out loud for fear of rejection, judgment, or abandonment.

When I got home, Stephen and I went for a run. I stopped halfway up a hill, turned to him, and said, "I'm an alcoholic." He looked at me with tears in both our eyes and said, "Finally, now we can move on." There was never any judgement or shame when I admitted it, only forward momentum. I never drank again from that day forward.

On that day, I came to terms with my toxic anchor. I realized almost everything I did was to make myself feel accepted by everyone else. Why? Because I didn't accept myself.

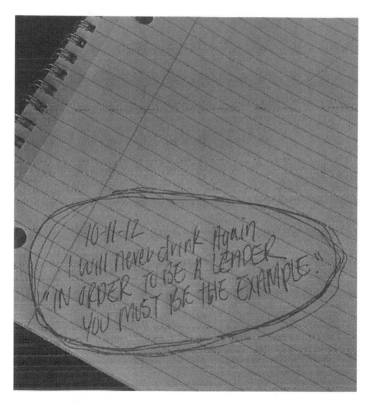

I wrote the date, the quote, and the statement that changed my life.

I had to learn to stop being afraid of finding out who I really was without having alcohol to hide behind. Making a change is hard. Sticking to it is even harder. And, maintaining openness with ourselves and other people without something to hide behind might be the hardest. That is why most of us go back to our toxic cycle and to doing things that don't make us feel good, the things we know are hurting us. It's easier to just give in.

Whatever our issues are, whether food or drugs, shopping or sex, they are all rooted in a **lack of self-acceptance and self-love combined with fear.** We look to unhealthy habits and people to fill those voids. It's impossible to learn how to love yourself from the approval of other people. Could you imagine if we stop filling our voids and instead focused on finding out who we really are?

There is a direct correlation between the happiness and success I've found in my life today and the decision I made to start loving myself and accepting myself just as I am. What I used to think defined me was, in reality, what was holding me back.

Whatever you're going through, it is not too big or too small. Whatever you're fighting, whatever is holding you down, holding you back, now is the moment you can cut the rope to your toxic anchor. It won't be easy, but it will be worth it.

We should all not just like who we are, we should LOVE who we are! You are amazing, and you deserve to be living you true potential. Once you do, you will realize that your happiness is more important than what other people think of you. It is through acceptance, respect, and self-love that we learn to stop filling the voids, face them, and change our lives.

THE WORK

1. What is your toxic anchor?

2. **Can you tell someone?**

(Call them. Ask them over for lunch. Say it out loud.)

3. Are you ready to cut the rope?

15

Starting a New Life

The day I admitted out loud to my business partner and myself that I was an alcoholic was the day everything changed, including my relationship with Stephen and our business. In our business relationship, I was the "talent," and Stephen was the marketing/business guy. We made an outstanding team. Our dynamic was so good that our business began growing faster than we knew what to do with it.

I was renting space at a gym and my classes were getting so big that it was annoying other trainers. Stephen had been successful in his own career as a designer, and after twenty-five years in that business, he also wanted a change. That was when he and I decided to go all in as 50/50 partners in a business of our own.

We found a vacant building in Santa Barbara and decided to open our own place there. A lot of people questioned Stephen's intentions. Many asked, "Why would a guy seventeen years older than Jenny want to make a career change at forty-eight years old, and did he just come in and fund it all? The greatest gift Stephen ever gave me was making me believe in and invest in myself as well as hand over my entire life savings.

It was December 2012, when everyone else was thinking about the holidays that I sat outside an empty room writing a check on the hood of my car a check that left me with only $75 in my checking account. I handed it over to him and said, "Are you going to lose this?" He looked me square in the eye and said, "I can't promise that, but I can promise you three things:"

1. You are going to help a lot of people.

2. We are going to have a lot of fun.

3. No matter what happens, you just made the best investment you will ever make. You invested in yourself.

It is an incredible thing to have someone believe in you, but it's an even bigger thing when you believe in yourself enough to make a leap. That day was one of the scariest and most pivotal days of my life.

My life changed drastically in that moment. I now know how to take responsibility for my actions and how to be honest with myself and others. I stopped looking at the big picture and instead chose to take it day by day. I also realized I am not unlucky, nor do bad things ever just *happen* to me. They happened because I was making toxic choices. Every action has a reaction.

I started to put one foot in front of the other and go day by day. Deciding to stay sober, deciding to go to work, deciding not to lie to others or myself, and starting to trust myself by letting go of what everyone else thought. I found the magic pill that everyone is looking for, and here it is:

Take action on a daily basis, in small doable steps. We have to stop looking so far into the future that it paralyzes us from taking the next step.

Whenever I would think about never drinking again, it would make me want to drink. Thoughts of how would I go to a party, how to spend holidays with family, how to go on a date and the thought not having alcohol ironically drove me to alcohol.

We have to trust the process, break it down and start now. Not on Monday. Not after your birthday. It starts now because waiting hasn't worked for you in the past. Make it small, whatever it is. Maybe it's not drinking today, deleting the Amazon app off your phone, or going for a walk after dinner instead of sitting on the couch bingeing on ice cream.

It doesn't have to mean forever. Just start where you are. You don't have to stop shopping forever or go for a three-mile walk right away. Maybe you can start with just five minutes around the block. Or committing for one day to saying no instead of yes to all the people who ask you to do the things you say yes to when you really want to say no.

This book is about changing your story and DOING THE WORK. You have to do the work in order to make real change. The work doesn't have to be overwhelming or so big that you feel defeated and stop. Make the work smaller and more doable. Take the small steps. Set yourself up for the win, just for today, because all you need is one step in the right direction.

I did not change my life overnight. It did not happen because I suddenly decided I was going to stop my toxic behaviors. It changed because I saw that I needed to heal myself and change my story. When I started to take the steps toward this, it began to happen. It has been more than worth it. I had the same issues as many of you. If I am able to do it, so can you.

Picture of me signing the check in the amount of my life savings

THE WORK

1. Do you believe in yourself and are you ready to make a change? Whether the answer is yes or no, why?

2. **What is one thing you can do today to start that change?**

3. **Who is one person who believes in you, does not enable you, and pushes you to be your best self? What do you want to say to them?**

    (An example of this person in my life was Stephen.)

16
Coming into My Own

When Stephen and I opened our own space, we agreed we didn't want to just open a gym. We wanted to start a community. Our intention was to create a place where people of all ages, athletic abilities, shapes, and sizes could come and feel welcomed. We wanted a place where there was no judgement, and it didn't matter if you were twenty-five or seventy-five. This was a place where everyone belonged. Whether you were a triathlete who runs a six-minute mile or someone who weighs four hundred pounds and is going to the gym for the first time. It was a place where everyone was side by side, high-fiving, encouraging, and supporting one another. No matter what. We wanted a place where people could let go of their stories and get back to finding themselves.

It was more than a "boot camp" or group fitness classes. It was a life-changing program. We created and named our gym the Jenny Schatzle Program, a six-week program with ten classes a day, a nutrition therapist, and a tagline that said, "Don't just change your body, change your life." People would join our six-week program in hopes of losing weight or getting in better shape, and what transpired in those six weeks was so much more.

The gym became their therapy, a place they could go and be a mom, co-worker, student, husband, or wife. They could release their problems of the day, anxiety, and stress and move in a place where they feel safe and not judged. We provided a place with great music, positive energy, and a community that supported each other.

At the end of each class, I gave a motivational speech, and with each speech you could see people's perspective starts to change. I talked about toxic anchors, toxic people, and how to accept, respect, and love yourself from the inside out, not the outside in.

Our program was built out of pure passion for wanting to help people feel good about themselves, and it worked. We were voted the most successful fitness business in Santa Barbara, and actually have held that title for the past five years.

Through the six years of building this business, which started out with just Stephen and I, we now have thirteen employees. Six trainers, four of whom work full-time for us with no side jobs, which is rare in a group fitness career, six front desk staff and a director of operations. We also have six front desk staff and a director of operations. This year, we rebranded to

Bond Fitness. Our tagline is, "We Get Fit Together." Our goal is to grow as a team, open more locations, and spread this message.

I've learned some important business and life lessons over the years. One of the most important was learning how to say no. Back in my people-pleasing days, I thought that the more I did for people, the more they would like me. I would give things away for free, like meal plans, classes, and entire programs. It wasn't until Stephen asked, "Why don't you value yourself?" that the light bulb turned on. He said, "This is what you do for a living, this is your career! You are talented and you work hard! Why are you just giving it away for free? People don't value free." He was right.

I used to think giving things away for free would make people want to commit for longer, that they'd see the value in what we did and ultimately pay for it. But in reality, the more stuff you give away for free, the more people expect to get it discounted and just want even more for free.

People don't like you or love you more for the more you do for them. They will only keep asking and expecting you to continue doing for them.

In the beginning, I sought out people's approval so much that it was hurting our business and I was being taken advantage of. Stephen said it best, "Value comes when you truly invest in yourself." This was my career, my life's passion, my business, and I was giving it away. It was at this point that I learned to say no and started to hold myself to a higher standard.

When we know to our core that we are good

enough and worthy of success, we stop giving it away. We start saying no to the things and people that don't align with who we want to be and yes to the things and people who do. That is a true life change.

THE WORK

1. What have you been giving away?

(You don't have to own your business to answer this question. It could be your time, energy, happiness, etc.)

2. To whom have you been giving it?

3. **What change do you want to make with this person, business, or situation?**

17
Doing the Work Changes Everything

I am not going to tell you that my life is perfect now that I have quit drinking, because it's not. Healing my issues did not automatically make my life one in which I never have setbacks or challenges. I have them all the time, because that is life…for everyone! Old issues still come up sometimes. I feel insecure or feel a need to make everybody happy. My life, my business, and my marriage are exactly what I wanted, but that does not mean any of them are easy or perfect. Ever.

What *did* happen is, I have better skills to deal with it. I don't binge on pizza and vodka when I am upset or going through something. Because I am authentic and open about what I am facing or struggling with, I can turn to myself to decide the right way to handle it. Sometimes I ask people in my life for help or their advice. The most important thing is, I do not turn to my toxic behaviors the way I used to.

You are not always going to feel comfortable in every situation, and you need to realize that every chapter of your life is going to require a different version of you. It is okay to change and evolve. We are supposed to. It is a part of life. Growth scares people who don't want to change or don't know how. But I will tell you, we *all* have problems. It does not matter how much money somebody has or how great their marriage is. Life has ups and downs for everybody. You are no different. You don't have to pretend that you are perfect or that you never have issues.

When you can be open and honest about what you are going through is when you can turn to something other than your toxic behaviors. And, when you have the right people around you, they are going to be there for you. They won't criticize or judge you. They will want to help and support you. I used to hide in my apartment when I felt bad and get drunk or eat. Now, I will tell the people who care about me what I am going through. I am open and honest. And you know what? They completely understand and want to help me get through it.

This is why it is important that you surround yourself with the right people. There are going to be people who support you as well as people who do not. Some people can't admit their own problems; they are not going to accept that you have yours. When I stopped drinking, I lost a lot of friends. I handed out a lot of pink slips when I stopped people-pleasing.

When you cut ties to people who do not support you or aren't living the way you want to, you will find the right people. Maybe you won't have any friends left when you change. Join a group or take a class that has the people you want and need. Reach out to people who are doing what you want to do and connect with them. You will be surprised by how willing positive people are to help and connect with others. Surround yourself with people who are smarter, faster, and better than you. Find people who are working to change, just as you are.

There are going to be people you can't cut ties with, such as your family or co-workers. Think about how they trigger or upset you, and then make the decision that you will change your mind about how it affects you. My sister and I fight a lot. This used to be a real trigger for me. I can't change her. But what I *can* do is not participate in what upsets me. Ninety-nine percent of what people do is a reflection of how they feel about themselves, a reflection of their own issues. When you realize this, it becomes a lot easier to stop letting what other people do affect you.

You are going to constantly change, evolve, and have challenges because that is life. Build your community. Get around people who are like-minded. You can't change how some people treat you, but you can change how you react and how their behavior affects you.

My husband, Connor, and my twin girls, Hope and Haven.

THE WORK

1. Can you accept that you are going to constantly have challenges, change, and evolve?

2. What can you do to embrace this?

3. What kind of people do you want or need in your life to support you with this? Who triggers you in your life, and how can you change your mind about how their behavior affects you?

18

Moving Forward

It requires constant work to evolve. I don't wake up every day to cupcakes and roses now that I've quit drinking, have a successful business, and am married with twins. I'm not super positive, proclaiming "I love my body and I love my life" every single minute of every single day. That is not possible.

But what I *do* do is wake up every day committed to bettering myself, no longer telling myself the story that doesn't serve me the story that I'm not good enough, smart enough, thin enough, pretty enough. The story that makes me fall weak to peer pressure, the story that made me think I wasn't worthy of success, so I needed to give it away. The story that kept me in an abusive relationship. The story that I wasn't good enough for my dad to stay sober, and that I wasn't good enough to fix him. This is no longer my story. It was never mine to begin with, but now I am aware of it. Awareness is how we change our lives.

Hopefully by now, THE WORK has brought up some deep-rooted issues for you. I hope you have identified the story you took on as a child and have been living your adult life believing. I hope that you now realize that it was never your story. That you have identified your toxic anchor and the negative habits that you have used to cope or numb out from the story.

Now is the time we get to forgive. We forgive the person who created this story for us because they didn't know any better. If it was a parent, they did the best they could with what they knew. Most likely, they learned it from their own parents. When we can let go and have empathy, we allow ourselves to see that this story never had anything to do with us and everything to do with them. This is the first step in breaking toxic family cycles so as not to pass them on.

We also need to forgive ourselves. We also did not know better. We are doing the best we can with what we know. But now you know more. You no longer have to sit in your suffering. You get to move forward and say, "NOT TODAY!" to that negative voice in your head.

Nobody moves forward and thrives in life through guilt and shame. It's time to let it go and get clear and authentic with yourself and the people around you, about who you are, what you want, and what you are going through.

The longest relationship you are ever going to have is the one you have with yourself. It's not selfish to take care of yourself, to want to evolve yourself, or to make steps to change. It's actually your responsibility.

Here is how we are going to end this: the work now involves you moving forward in your life, releasing what no longer serves you, and going after what you really want.

These are the three things I do on a daily basis:

Change Your Daily I AM Statements

I did a whole TED Talk on this. I want you to think about the way you talk to yourself about yourself right now. Do you get out of the shower and say, "I am fat, I am old, I am wrinkly, I am broke, I am tired. I am not smart enough, I am not good enough"? You are what you say you are. So, starting today, I want you to write down or say to yourself every morning:

I am _____
I am _____
I am _____

Every morning I say to myself, "I am strong, I am smart, I am successful. I am kind. I am love. I am light." I usually can't stop at just three! Yours can be whatever you want them to be. You are not going to feel like you are these things every day, but the more you can pump positivity into your system, the more it will start to sink in.

Give the Negative Voice in Your Head a Name

Those negative thoughts that say, "You're fat, you're lazy, you shouldn't ask for the raise," the voice that keeps you locked in fear: NAME IT. It could be someone you don't particularly care for or just a random name like Jenny (haha). Give it a name so that when those thoughts come in, you have awareness that those thoughts do NOT serve you. Stop and say, "NOT TODAY, JENNY!" Then move on with your day. We all have negative thoughts. It's what we do with those thoughts that matters. It is only when you give them power and life that they have power and life. So, don't do it.

Journal

Do you go to bed with a "monkey mind" or a head that won't stop thinking, maybe some anxiety or thoughts of what or who has bothered you that day? Write it down. Especially if you can't sleep. Sit down for five minutes and write down everything you are thinking. It doesn't have to make sense. Just write. Or, maybe you write your to-do list for the next day. Even if you don't do what's on the list, write it out. Maybe write the good things you want to happen the next day to help your mind settle down.

Journaling of any kind, any time of day, helps. I personally do it first thing in the morning and before bed. In the morning, I write three things I am grateful for and my I AM statements. I also meditate with a smartphone app for five minutes. If you have been doing the work in this book, you have been journaling with the questions. Now keep it going! And remember, you don't have to follow any guide or rules. Do what feels right for you, when it feels right.

It is when we have awareness and tools that we are able to change. This book is just the beginning of the change. It's the first step in recognizing the deep-rooted story and the second step of releasing the story in order to live, expand, and own your truest self.

Your past is not your life sentence unless you allow it to be.

19

Thank You

This book has been one of the hardest things I have done. And, to be honest, it's taken me years to write. I was never good in school, I never considered myself a writer, and one of my toxic anchors was believing I wasn't smart enough or good enough to write an actual book. I let go of that story and decided that no matter what happens with this book, I am writing it because I believe our stories are important (all of our stories). If this book helps just one person, I have done my job.

I want to thank all the people in my life who believed in me even before I believed in myself. Transition in any form is hard, but when we realize we have the power to rewrite our story and that our past is not our life sentence, we put ourselves back in control of what we really want in life.

I believe in you, and now is the time for you to start believing in yourself.

Thank you for allowing me to share my story with you. I want to hear your story. I want to know about your progress, your toxic anchors, and your *aha* moments. Follow me on Instagram and sign up for my email list. Come to one of my talks or visit us at Bond Fitness.

I love all of you, and I am so excited to be on this journey together,

Jenny Schatzle

Acknowledgements

Thank you to everyone who has helped with my first book!

My husband, Connor. My business partner, Stephen. Patricia, my mom, my dad (R.I.P).

Dean, Teri, Rob, Laura, Caroline, Jack, Blake, My In-laws Beverly and Rick. The entire staff at Bond Fitness; Lauren, Chito, Jarratt, Shem, Beth, Cosmo, Aolani, Claire, Kelli, Grayson, Emma. All my girl-friends known as the The Sundays. Leela, my soul sister, and so many more. I know I've left some people out, but I cannot end without thanking the two great-est lessons I've had in my life, Hope and Haven.

About the Author

Jenny Schatzle doesn't change bodies, she changes lives! She is a wellness and lifestyle guide who helps people feel good about themselves. Her platform is about changing the conversation on self-worth, body image, and life perspective. She has created the hugely successful, life-changing Jenny Schatzle Program. Her passion is empowering people to accept themselves, respect themselves, and love themselves in every aspect of their lives. Jenny has created a movement that challenges the way people see themselves. Her program is as much about health and wellness as it is about positivity, self-love, and letting go of the behaviors and negative thinking that stop us and limit our success.

Jenny has been featured in dozens of media outlets worldwide and has given two TEDx Talks that had audiences on their feet. She's also been named the National Association of Women Business Owners (NAWBO) female business owner of the year. The mom of twin girls, she is an inspiration and example for men, women, families, and people everywhere. Through movement, media, and online programs, she's driving a new era of change with fitness, body image, and self-worth. Jenny helps people change the conversation about who they are, what they can do, and all they can be.

Made in the USA
Las Vegas, NV
03 December 2020